The Tramways of
South Wales

(Networks Edition)

This booklet is one of a series which sets down in a short form the history and geography of Britain's Tramways, enlarged from the regional chapters of *Great British Tramway Networks,* a book by W. H. Bett and J. C. Gillham which had four editions from 1942 to 1962 but has long been out of print. The present work originates in Chapter Eight of *Networks,* which dealt with South Wales and the Severn Estuary, but much more information has since come to light.

The district along the coast of South Wales forms a natural geographic unit whose huge mineral wealth led to vast industrial development in the 19th century. As in other such areas, this led to the development of street tramways, though the pattern of narrow valleys, largely isolated from one another, prevented much linking up. So although the area was well provided with tramway systems, none very far apart, there were only two instances of track connection and through running. The arrangement in this book is east-to-west, starting with Newport and then along the coast to Cardiff. From here we turn inland to visit Pontypridd, Rhondda, Aberdare, and Merthyr Tydfil, before returning to the coast at Neath and continuing westwards via Swansea and the Mumbles to Llanelly (spelt nowadays as Llanelli). We will also mention some proposed tramways that were not built, and some funiculars and narrow-gauge railways. Distances are shown in miles and chains, which was normal practice in tramway days, hence note that 80 chains equal one mile.

Newport

The easternmost tramway system was at Newport, then in Monmouthshire but now in Gwent. Here, the Newport (Mon) Tramways Co. Ltd. opened a 1m 13ch standard-gauge horse tramway from the town centre to the Docks area in 1875. This was purchased in 1894 by Newport Corporation, who built a further 3m 3ch and leased both to Solomon Andrews & Sons until 1901. The Corporation electrified the system in 1903 (except a short branch along Church Road), extending the Malpas Road, Caerleon Road, and Chepstow Road routes, and adding new routes along Corporation Road and to Stow Hill. The 1875 route was extended in 1917 from Pill (short for Pillgwenlly) to the Alexandra North Dock gates, after the Ministry of

COVER PICTURE: A Swansea and Mumbles steam train at Brynmill, about 1912. The nearest car is one of four built by Milnes of Hadley (Shropshire) in 1902 and designed for conversion to an electric tram if and when the line was electrified. Instead of this, they ran as steam-hauled trailers for 27 years. *(Courtesy P. Trotter)*

Newport bogie car 51 crossing the new Town Bridge across the River Usk in May 1927, during a two-week period in which eastbound trams still used the temporary wooden bridge erected in 1922. *(Lens of Sutton*

Munitions had persuaded the Great Western Railway to allow the trams to cross a busy five-track level crossing. Some 26 horse, and 58 electric cars of six types, were used, but Corporation motor buses replaced two routes in 1928/30 and four in 1937. A proposed extension of the Corporation Road route would have taken the trams to a point near Newport's transporter bridge, built in 1906 and owned by the County Council. Closed since 1985, this prominent local landmark is now being repaired.

In 1930 Newport Corporation obtained an Act for trolleybuses along and beyond the Chepstow Road tramway to the Royal Oak and Christchurch Village, but motor buses were used instead. In 1911 the Western Valleys (Monmouthshire) Railless Electric Traction Company promoted a Bill for a 20-mile trolleybus route from Newport's Stow Hill tram terminus via Risca, Abercarn, Crumlin, Blaina, and Nantyglo to Brynmawr. Only the eight miles from Llanhilleth to Brynmawr were authorised, plus three short branches at Abertillery in 1913, but the Great War killed this scheme.

Cardiff

The city of Cardiff was well suited to tramway operation, with fairly wide streets and negligible gradients. Horse buses of many owners were joined in 1872 by the horse trams of the Cardiff Tramways Co. Ltd., a member of the Provincial Tramways group which also had tramways at Plymouth, Portsmouth, and Grimsby. Extensions in Cardiff brought Provincial into conflict with the main bus owner, Solomon Andrews, who built new buses that fitted the tram tracks. A separate Cardiff District and Penarth Harbour Tramway Co. Ltd. opened a 2m 33ch line in 1881 from Adamsdown to Grangetown, operated by Andrews on their behalf, but Provincial bought Andrews's Cardiff tramway interests early in 1888. Cardiff Corporation took over the CTC lines in January 1902 and the Penarth line a year later, and quickly electrified and extended them, introducing 94 electric trams in less than a year.

All Cardiff trams were designed to pass under low railway bridges, 30 being single-deckers for the Salisbury Road and Grangetown-Splott routes, and 100 being low-built open-toppers. In 1923-25 Cardiff introduced 81 covered-top cars specially designed to fit under 15ft bridges, with well-type underframes and small wheels and motors, but 31 new single-deckers bought in 1926-27 were replaced by buses in 1936 and sold in 1940 to Para in Brazil. In 1942 all Cardiff trams were fitted with Pay-As-You-Enter equipment, whereby passengers put one penny in the slot of a glass-sided fare box on boarding, and could then ride any distance without receiving a ticket. The fare was raised to 1½d in 1949, but the PAYE system and flat fare were discontinued a year later. Replacement by trolleybuses began on the Clarence Road-Cathedral Road route in 1942 and was completed in 1947-50. A proposed 2⅛ mile tramway extension of 1927 from Victoria Park to Ely, which would have had a reserved sleeper track along Grand Avenue, was built as a trolleybus route in 1955, but motor buses replaced all Cardiff trolleybuses in 1962-70.

Penarth and Barry

Despite the second Cardiff company's title its trams never reached Penarth, and the Penarth Tramway Syndicate Limited was later formed in 1903 to build an electric tramway from Grangetown to Penarth town centre, with a branch to Dinas Powis, totalling 4m 26ch. Five miles beyond Penarth is Barry, where in 1893 the Barry Railway Company obtained an Act for 3ft 6in gauge horse tramways from Barry Town Station to Whitmore Bay on Barry Island, 1m 11ch, with a 34ch branch along Plymouth Road. But in 1894 a new Act authorised most of this to be built instead as a railway, which was opened in 1896 and is still in use today.

Prototype Cardiff lowbridge tram 101 passing under the ex-Taff Vale bridge in Queen Street on 23 August 1939, seen from the ex-Rhymney Railway bridge. Mr. Priestley obtained GWR permission to photograph from both bridges. *(H. B. Priestley*

Pontypridd

North-west of Cardiff we reach the typical Welsh valleys, of which the best known is the Rhondda, formerly served by the most extensive tramway system in Wales. The Pontypridd & Rhondda Valley Tramways Company was authorised in 1882 to make 12m 30ch of 3ft 6in horse tramway from Pontypridd via Trehafod, Porth, Pen-y-graig, Tonypandy, Llwyn-y-pia, Ystrad-y-fodwg, and Treorchy to Treherbert. This would have been probably the longest horse tramway anywhere in Britain, but most of it was dropped and only the first 3m 9ch was built, from Pontypridd to Porth, and was worked by Solomon Andrews & Sons. This was purchased in 1899 by the British Electric Traction Co. Ltd., who applied in 1900 for powers to electrify it and extend it to Cilfynydd and Tonypandy. The Pontypridd and Rhondda Urban District Councils both objected to this, but an epidemic in February 1902 killed most of the horses so the service was reduced to two workmen's cars each morning and evening. The full service was never resumed, and the two councils each bought half of the line from the BET in 1904, splitting it at Trehafod.

Pontypridd UDC built and opened electric tramways to Cilfynydd and Treforest in 1905, with a depot at Glyntaff. When their Trehafod section was electrified in 1907 it was unconnected to the main route, due to viaduct construction, and its single-deck cars were kept in a small shed at Trehafod. By the time the tracks were connected the route had been cleared for double-deck cars, leaving little work for the single-deckers. From May 1919 Pontypridd and Rhondda tramcars worked a joint service between Pontypridd and Porth, and some Company cars ran through to the Rhondda valleys, providing one of only two instances of Welsh through running. From Pontypridd centre to near Treforest the electric trams followed the course of an 1809 mineral tramway which took coal from Trehafod to a canal wharf at Treforest. A two-mile electric extension from Treforest along the Cardiff road to Upper Boat was

TRAMWAY NETWORKS IN ACTION

Left: **Pontypridd No. 7 and two Rhondda trams at Porth. Joint through running continued until 1931.** *(Dr. Hugh Nicol)*

Right: **Swansea 38 and a Swansea & Mumbles car at St. Helens in June 1936.** *(G. N. Southerden)*

authorised in 1920, but not built. Pontypridd abandoned its Trehafod tramway in 1931 and replaced the other two by trolleybuses, and new road construction has since obliterated most of the route to Cilfynydd.

Rhondda

After Rhondda UDC had purchased its half of the BET tramway beyond the end-on junction at Trehafod it leased this to the National Electric Construction Co. Ltd., which also owned tramways at Oxford, Torquay, Ossett, Mexborough, and Musselburgh. In 1906 the newly-formed Rhondda Tramways Co. Ltd. took over the lease from its parent NEC, electrifying the route in 1908 and extending it in 1908 and 1912. From Porth the electric tramway followed the 1882 horse proposal to Treherbert and Blaen-Rhondda at the head of the main valley, with, as far as Llwyn-y-pia, another route on the opposite side of the valley, also a branch from Pen-y-graig to Williamstown, but the authorised branch to Clydach Vale was not built. Another line in a tributary valley ran roughly parallel from Porth through Tylorstown and Ferndale to Maerdy. Thus 54 cars of both open and closed-top types worked 20m 73ch of 3ft 6in route, all being leased from the Rhondda UDC. The trams suffered greatly from mining subsidence, also from single track and passing loops, of which there were 52 on the Porth via Tonypandy to Blaen-Rhondda route. Through-running with Pontypridd's municipal tramways worked from 1919 until 1931, but the entire Rhondda system was replaced by diesel buses early in 1934.

The Rhondda Tramways Co. Ltd. also ran trolleybuses, but not for very long. A 4m 63ch trolleybus route from Williamstown to Gilfach Goch via Tonyrefail and Gilfach was opened at the end of 1914, but ceased three months later due to road subsidence. This was in the area of the Llantrisant & Llantwit Fardre Rural District Council, who were empowered in 1920 to build a 3ft 6in gauge tramway along the same 4m 59ch route, to be leased to the Rhondda company, but this was not built. The two villages from which this area's Council took its name were six miles away to the south-east, and the Rhondda later grew into a large bus operator.

Aberdare

Mid-way between the Rhondda and Merthyr, but cut off from both by the intervening mountains, is the town of Aberdare, where the UDC obtained tramway powers in 1911 for a 3ft 6in line from Trecynon through Aberdare to Aberaman, opened in 1913. An extension from Trecynon to Hirwaun was rejected in 1915, but in 1914 four short trolleybus routes totalling 4m 63ch were opened to Cwmdare, Abernant, Cwmaman, and Capcoch, using the over-running Cedes-Stoll system of current collection, the trolleybuses being towed to and from the depot at Gadlys by tram. In 1921-22 the Cwmaman and Capcoch routes were replaced by new tramways, with an extension to Abercwmboi, whilst motorbuses replaced the Cwmdare trolleybuses in 1922 and Abernant in 1925. In the next few years the Council expanded its bus services, and they replaced the trams in 1935.

Further down the Cynon valley Mountain Ash UDC applied unsuccessfully in 1902 for powers for a 5m 13ch tramway from Abercwmboi to Abercynon, which is only two miles north of Cilfynydd, and, with Hirwaun and Treforest, could have led to a 16-mile through route.

Merthyr Tydfil

Three miles north-east of Abernant, but isolated from it by a 1364-foot high mountain road, is Merthyr Tydfil, where the Merthyr Electric Traction & Lighting Co. Ltd. (a BET subsidiary) had 3m 40ch of 3ft 6in gauge line from Graham Street,

Merthyr, to Cefn Coed and to Dowlais (Bush Inn), including a 42ch extension of 1914 beyond Cefn Bridge. There was once a vast steelworks at Dowlais, which provided a heavy workmen's traffic in the prosperous days of South Wales. The Dowlais route climbed 341 feet in little over a mile, partly at 1-in-11, and was originally restricted to single-deck cars. The average width of the streets used by Merthyr's trams was only 23ft, and the narrowest section, at Portmorlais, a mere 14ft 8ins. Narrow roads prevented any extension further south. The depot and power station was on the site of the 1784 Pen-y-daren Ironworks, where Trevithick made pioneer locomotive experiments in 1804. Merthyr Corporation considered purchasing the company in 1911, and using trolleybuses from Dowlais to Pant, 2 miles, and Merthyr to Treharris, 7½ miles, but nothing came of this. Latterly the Company fleet was mostly secondhand Birmingham trams with their top covers removed, and, despite its smallness, it was not abandoned until 1939, when municipal motorbuses took over, leaving the Company to continue with electricity supply until 1948. The 1901 to 1939 spread of electric trams was the longest in South Wales except at Cardiff.

Aberavon

So far we have studied the valleys which run nearly parallel in a south-easterly direction converging on Cardiff, but other valleys run south-westwards towards Neath and Swansea, the two groups forming roughly an inverted V, whose apex encloses many collieries but no large towns or tramways. Back on the coastal plain the Aberavon District Tramways Syndicate, Limited, of Newport, Mon., was empowered in 1905 to build 3m 66ch of tramway from Aberavon through Port Talbot to Margam. This was never built, but probably would have been if today's huge steelworks at Margam had been opened earlier than it was.

Neath and Briton Ferry

At the foot of the Vale of Neath was the 3m 77ch standard-gauge horse tramway of the Neath & District Tramways Co. Ltd., opened in 1875 from Briton Ferry through Neath to Skewen. Neath Corporation bought the line by Act of 1897, which also authorised electrification and 77ch of new routes which were not built. Instead of electrification the line was leased to the British Gas Traction Co. Ltd. (succeeded in 1902 by the Provincial Gas Traction Co. Ltd.), who used gas-engined cars, some of which came secondhand in 1903 from the Blackpool, St. Annes, & Lytham Tramways Company. The lease was surrendered in 1916, and Neath Corporation ran the gas cars until 1920, when it retired from transport, after furnishing one of the only three examples on the mainland of Britain (with Matlock and Morecambe) of a municipal tramway system which was never electrified. Buses of the South Wales Transport Co. Ltd. then took over.

Earlier, in 1879, a Briton Ferry & Swansea Tramway Company obtained an Act for 4m 45ch of tramway from the Ferry House Hotel on the west bank of the River Neath estuary opposite Briton Ferry, via Crymlyn Burrows, well to the south of Jersey Marine Hotel, and Lockwood Bridge, to end at Port Tennant, 26 years before the Swansea tramways reached Port Tennant from the opposite direction, but this was never built.

Swansea

At Skewen the Neath tramway was less than four miles from the nearest part of the standard-gauge Swansea tramway system, which was worked by a company established in 1874, the Swansea Improvements & Tramways Company. This is a

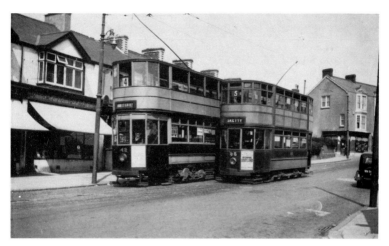

Swansea 42 and 35 at Sketty terminus, June 1936. No. 35 was Swansea's newest tram, built in 1933.   *(G. N. Southerden*

most invidious title, for is not a tramway an improvement to any town? (In fact this referred to street widenings). The SI&T built and owned horse tramways which opened from College Street to St. Helens and to Morriston (Copper Platform) in 1878 and to Cwmbwrla in 1882. Cwmbwrla was steam-worked at first, and all three were electrified in 1900. The Brynmill, Sketty, Port Tennant, and Brynhyfryd lines, and the Morriston route continuation to Tircanol, were opened in 1905 and owned by Swansea Corporation but leased to the SI&T. A further 49ch beyond Tircanol Post Office to Ynysforgan was owned by Glamorgan County Council, who obtained powers in 1903 totalling 5m 67ch to extend it via Clydach and Pontardawe to Craig Llangiwg, but these were not used, and the Morriston-Ynysforgan section was replaced by motorbuses in 1933. The other routes were similarly treated in 1937, the buses being owned by SI&T but operated by the South Wales Transport Co. Ltd., a fellow-member of the BET group.

The Swansea tram fleet was a very varied assortment, with some cars obtained secondhand from four other systems, but their origins were concealed by very thorough rebuilding in the 1920's. Single-deckers ran the eastern route to Port Tennant and the northern routes to Morriston, Brynhyfryd, and Cwmbwrla, although double-deckers could run as far as the low railway bridge just short of Cwmbwrla terminus. In 1923 a bridge at Landore was altered to allow double-deckers to run to Morriston, these being lowbridge cars of the type newly adopted in Cardiff. Ordinary double-deckers worked the other routes to Sketty, Brynmill, and St. Helens. For many years the fleet size remained constant at 79 units, but most of these latterly had replaced others scrapped earlier.

From 1898 to 1901 a short 14ch 3ft 6in gauge cable tramway in the form of a street funicular was operated by the Swansea Constitution Hill Incline Tramway Co. Ltd. up a steep hill to Mount Pleasant in the western part of Swansea, but it had no connection with the electric lines. The winding gear was powered by a gas engine, but an overhead wire was used for signalling purposes, with steepest gradient 1 in 3½, average 1-in-5, and two 18-seat cars by Brush.

Mumbles

The Swansea and Mumbles Railway ran round the edge of Swansea Bay to Mumbles Pier, and could trace its history back to the almost unbelievable date of 1804. It was originally a mineral line owned by the Oystermouth Railway or Tramroad Company, and achieved the distinction of becoming the first passenger railway in the world by allowing a contractor to run a horse-drawn coach in March 1807. Originally the line started at The Cwm, near where the GWR station was later built in 1850, and ran along The Strand and Victoria Road, but this part became disused and was later leased to the Swansea Harbour Trust. For all the rest of its life the terminus was at Rutland Street, where direct physical connection with the LNWR and GWR was available, also indirectly to the Midland. In 1877 the Oystermouth line carried the second regular British steam tramway service, one year after Wantage, interspersed with through SI&T horse trams from Gower Street which used a connecting track at St. Helens until 1896. The extension from Oystermouth to Mumbles Pier was opened in stages in 1894-98, and a 999-year lease of the whole line was taken in 1899 by the SI&T Company. During the next 30 years heavy excursion traffic was carried by trains of up to a dozen double-deck open-top tramway-type cars, pulled by a steam locomotive. The lease was transferred in 1927 to the South Wales Transport Co. Ltd., one of the largest bus operators in Wales.

The depot was at Rutland Street terminus, and from here the line ran along the edge of the highway, unpaved and unfenced, later leaving the road and running on the very edge of the sea only a few feet from high-water mark. Hence the trams, both steam and the later electric, had all their entrances on the landward side. Electrification did not occur until 1928 (opened 1929), when covered-top all-enclosed cars, the largest anywhere in Britain and seating 106, were introduced. They were equipped for multiple-unit control, with continuous air brakes and pantograph collectors. The route length was 5m 30ch, and the electric cars stopped at only eight intermediate points, taking only 19 minutes. The bus company still seemed very proud of its Mumbles railway when in 1954 it celebrated, in very grand style, its 150th anniversary, but it had in fact changed its opinion, and abandoned the line at the beginning of 1960 at the ripe old age of 155. As the lease was not due to expire until the year 2898 the operating company had first to purchase the two companies which owned the line. These were the Swansea and Mumbles Railway, Limited, of 1879, for the Swansea end, and the Mumbles Railway and Pier Company formed in 1889, both of which were dissolved by the 1959 Act which sanctioned abandonment.

The Mumbles line had one branch, the Clyne Valley Mineral Railway, which diverged to the right between Ashleigh Road and Blackpill Halts to serve

To mark the 150th anniversary of the incorporation of the Oystermouth Railway or Tramroad Company in 1804, the Swansea & Mumbles Railway built this replica horse-drawn coach in 1954 to represent the first passenger vehicle, Simon Llewellyn's coach of 1807. It is now in the Swansea Maritime and Industrial Museum.

(J. H. Price

A crowded steam train leaving Swansea for Mumbles Pier, about 1912. The centre car
is a former battery car.   (Courtesy P. Trotter

Rhydydyfyd Colliery, and also saw occasional race specials and Sunday School
excursions composed entirely of open carriages. Continuing on beyond here, the
Gower Light Railway, promoted in 1896 by Colonel H. F. Stephens, of Tonbridge,
Kent, was empowered to extend westwards for 12m 66ch via Killay and Llanrhidian
to Port Eynon, with running powers over the S&M, but construction did not
proceed.

Llanelly

Across the neck of the Gower Peninsula lies Llanelly, 9 or 10 miles distant from
Port Eynon or Black Pill or four of the Swansea termini. Here a company in the
Balfour Beatty group had three tramways extending from the railway station to Pwll,
Felinfoel, and Bynea. From 1882 until the electric cars began the one-mile route
from the Station to the town centre was worked by the 3ft 0in gauge horse trams of
the Llanelly Tramways Co. Ltd., with five single-deck cars and 13 horses. The
company was purchased in 1900 by the Llanelly & District Electric Lighting &
Traction Co. Ltd., which became the L&D Electric Supply Co. Ltd. in 1924. For the
last year or two prior to the 1911 electrification three ex-London horse cars worked
a service on 1m 8ch of the new standard-gauge tracks. The electric system was mainly
single track, partly with electric signals. The trams were replaced by trolleybuses in
the winter of 1932-33, and the overhead was extended beyond Bynea to Loughor
Bridge only six miles from Cwmbwrla (Swansea), bringing the total to 8m 30ch. In
1937 powers were obtained to extend another 5m 30ch to Burry Port and Pembrey,
but the road widening was deferred and then cancelled. The company was always a
supplier of domestic and industrial electricity, right out to Kidwelly, and in 1925 it

bought the Gorseinon Electric Light Co. Ltd. Following nationalisation of the electricity industry in 1948 the trolleybuses were replaced in 1952 by South Wales motor buses, whilst in 1967 the town changed its name from Llanelly to Llanelli.

Other lines

South Wales has two narrow-gauge tourist railways, the 60cm-gauge Brecon Mountain Railway of 1980 from Pant (north of Merthyr Tydfil) to the Taf Fechan reservoir at Pontsticill, and the 2ft-gauge Teifi Valley Railway from Henllan to Llandyfriog near Newcastle Emlyn opened in 1986. The seaside resort of Porthcawl had a 15-inch-gauge railway at Coney Beach from 1932 to 1936, and there is a similar line at Saundersfoot. A temporary 3ft 6in gauge funicular railway was at the Welsh Garden Festival at Ebbw Vale in 1992.

In Heath Park at Cardiff is the layout operated by the Whitchurch & District Model Engineering Society, with a miniature railway and an 18-inch-gauge electric tramway which has two passenger trams and an electric locomotive. Established at Heath Junction in 1973 as the Highfield Electric Tramway, it moved to its present site in 1987. Surviving full-size trams are a Cardiff horse car in the Welsh Industrial and Maritime Museum at Cardiff docks, a recently-rebuilt gas tram at Neath, a Swansea double-decker, a Mumbles 1807 replica, and one end of a Mumbles electric car, all in the Swansea Maritime and Industrial Museum, and Cardiff's rail-grinder in the National Tramway Museum's off-site store in Derbyshire. Finally, in the autumn of 1992 British Rail announced they were studying the possible conversion of their Cardiff Valleys network to electric rail operation, in conjunction with the Cardiff Bay Development Corporation.

The late Mr. Felix Cunuder, former chief engineer of Cardiff City Transport, driving car No. 1 of the 18-inch gauge Heath Park Electric Tramway on the official opening day, 5 September 1987. The passengers included the Lord Mayor of Cardiff. *(A. Bird*

NEWPORT

Newport horse
tram 6 at the High
Street terminus of
the Malpas Road
service.   *(TMS*

Newport 37 and
49 at the depot in
1934. No. 49 was
one of six cars
brought from the
London County
Council in 1917
and reduced in
height at Newport.
*(Dr. H. A. Whitcombe
courtesy Science
Museum*

Newport 57 of
1922 at Corpora-
tion Road terminus
in 1934.
*(Dr. H. A. Whitcombe
courtesy Science
Museum*

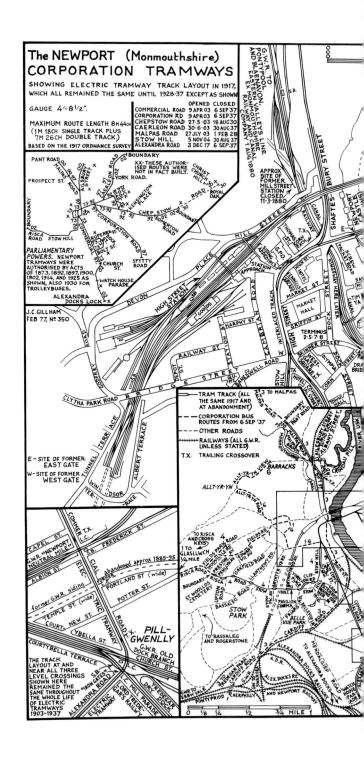

The NEWPORT (Monmouthshire) CORPORATION TRAMWAYS

SHOWING ELECTRIC TRAMWAY TRACK LAYOUT IN 1917, WHICH ALL REMAINED THE SAME UNTIL 1928-37 EXCEPT AS SHOWN

GAUGE 4'-8½".

MAXIMUM ROUTE LENGTH 8M 44CH (1M 18CH SINGLE TRACK PLUS 7M 26CH DOUBLE TRACK.)
BASED ON THE 1917 ORDNANCE SURVEY

	OPENED	CLOSED
COMMERCIAL ROAD	9 APR 03	6 SEP 37
CORPORATION RD	9 APR 03	6 SEP 37
CHEPSTOW ROAD	27·5·03	18 AUG 30
CAERLEON ROAD	30·6·03	30 AUG 37
MALPAS ROAD	27 JLY 03	1 FEB 28
STOW HILL	5 NOV 04	30 AUG 37
ALEXANDRA ROAD	3 DEC 17	6 SEP 37

PARLIAMENTARY POWERS. NEWPORT TRAMWAYS WERE AUTHORISED BY ACTS OF 1873, 1892, 1897, 1900, 1902, 1914, AND 1925 AS SHOWN, ALSO 1930 FOR TROLLEYBUSES.

J.C.GILLHAM FEB 77, No 350

XX - THESE AUTHORISED ROUTES WERE NOT IN FACT BUILT.

E - SITE OF FORMER EAST GATE
W - SITE OF FORMER WEST GATE

TRAM TRACK (ALL THE SAME 1917 AND AT ABANDONMENT)
CORPORATION BUS ROUTES FROM 6 SEP '37
OTHER ROADS
RAILWAYS (ALL G.W.R. UNLESS STATED)
T.X.   TRAILING CROSSOVER

THE TRACK LAYOUT AT AND NEAR ALL THREE LEVEL CROSSINGS SHOWN HERE REMAINED THE SAME THROUGHOUT THE WHOLE LIFE OF ELECTRIC TRAMWAYS 1903-1937

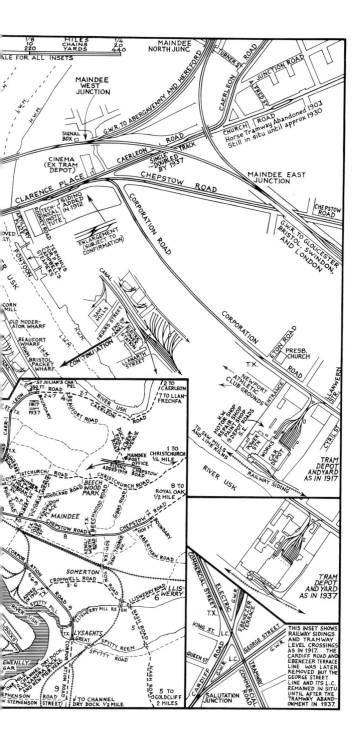

Newport 28 (as rebuilt in 1928) at the Docks terminus in 1934. This was the only Newport open-top car to receive a top cover.

(G. N. Southerden

Front-exit bogie car Newport 52 in High Street on the Post Office—Corporation Road service. Nos. 51-54 were built by Brush in 1921.

(G. N. Southerden

A close-up view of the 1906 Transporter Bridge across the River Usk at Newport, seen from the east tower. The trolley is just visible in the lower right-hand corner.

(Commercial postcard

CARDIFF

Cardiff Tramways Company horse car 24 at the Roath Broadway terminus of the Newport Road route. These cars had folding (instead of sliding) bulkhead doors.
(National Museum of Wales

Cardiff Corporation single-decker 46 of series 41-54 in St. Mary Street about 1904, on the service to Cathays.
Commercial postcard

One of Cardiff Corporation's original 1902 bogie cars, No. 37, at the original Roath Park stub-end terminus. All Cardiff trams were designed to pass under the many low railway bridges.
(Courtesy A. D. Packer

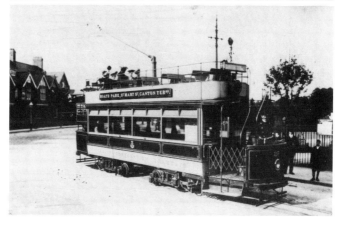

18

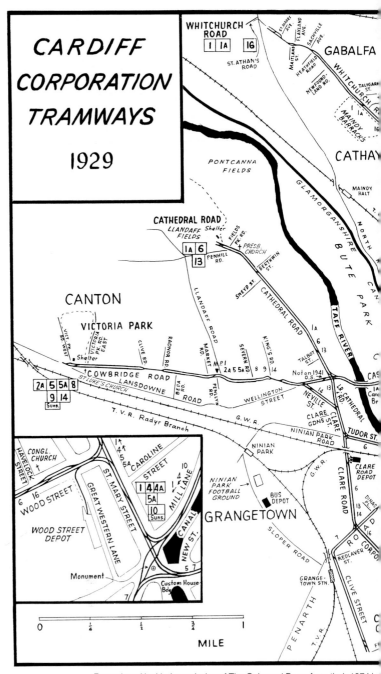

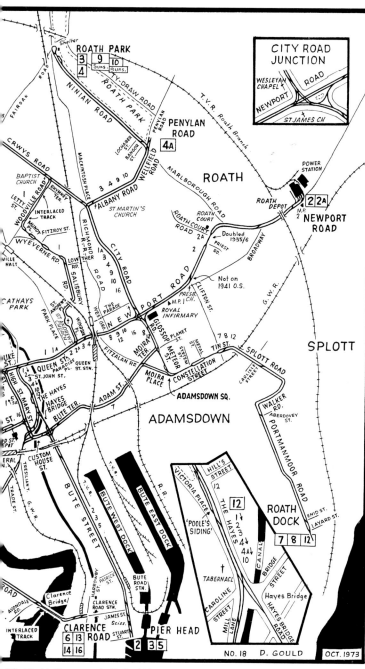

...diff's Electric Tramways, by D. Gould (second edition in preparation).

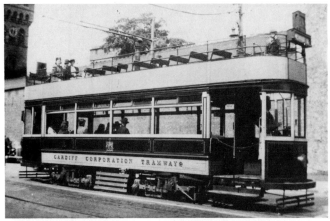

CARDIFF

Rebuilt bogie car 29 passing Cardiff Castle on 25 August 1940.
(J. C. Gillham

Roath depot on 15 April 1939, with the 1926/27 single-deck cars stored pending sale. The centre vehicle is the track-cleaning car.
(H. B. Priestley

Builder's interior view of Cardiff single-deck Car 50 of 1927, showing the cane rattan seats. These cars were sold in 1940 to Para in Brazil.
(Tramway & Railway World

The standard Cardiff trams in later years were these 64-seat low bridge enclosed cars of which there were 81. This photograph is of No. 80 in wartime grey livery, with masked headlamp and white fender, at Whitchurch Road terminus on 5 July 1945. A 'PAYE' board inside the windscreen refers to Cardiff's pay-as-you-enter system. At that time there was a universal penny fare on Cardiff's trams. *(D. W. Winkworth*

Cardiff 2 and 114 in Bute Terrace on 4 February 1950. This line, disused since 1936, was reopened in July 1949, as a diversion route to allow Queen Street to be lowered beneath the railway bridge for double-deck trolley buses. *(J. H. Meredith*

22

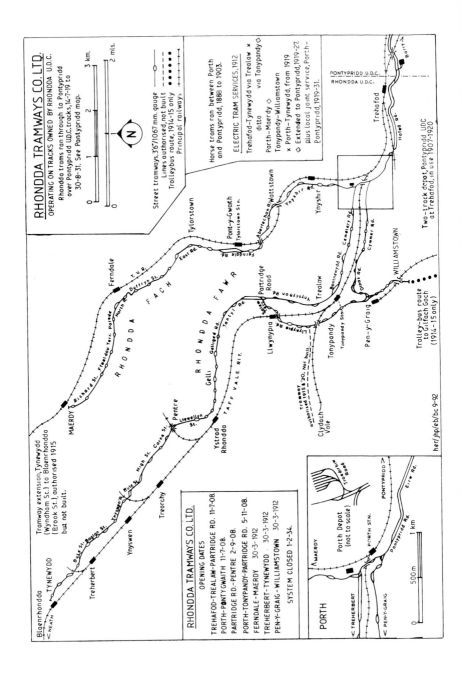

RHONDDA TRAMWAYS CO. LTD.

OPERATING ON TRACKS OWNED BY RHONDDA U.D.C.

Rhondda trams ran through to Pontypridd over Pontypridd U.D.C.tracks, 14-7-19 to 30-8-31. See Pontypridd map.

Street tramways, 3'6"/1067 mm. gauge — — — —
Lines authorised, not built
Trolleybus route, 1914-15 only
Principal railways

Horse trams ran between Porth and Pontypridd, 1888 to 1903.

ELECTRIC TRAM SERVICES, 1912

Trehafod-Tynewydd via Treolow ×
ditto   via Tonypandy ◇
Porth-Maerdy ◇
Tonypandy-Williamstown
× Porth-Tynewydd, from 1919
◇ Extended to Pontypridd,1919-27,
plus local joint service, Porth-
Pontypridd,1919-31.

PONTYPRIDD U.D.C.
RHONDDA U.D.C.

Two-track depot, Pontypridd UDC
at Trehafod, in use 1907-1920

herl/jhp/eb/bc 9-92

RHONDDA TRAMWAYS CO. LTD.
OPENING DATES

TREHAFOD-TREALAW-PARTRIDGE RD. 11-7-08.
PORTH-PONTYGWAITH 11-7-08.
PARTRIDGE RD.-PENTRE 2-9-08.
PORTH-TONYPANDY-PARTRIDGE RD. 5-11-08.
FERNDALE-MAERDY 30-3-1912
TREHERBERT-TYNEWYDD 30-3-1912
PEN-Y-GRAIG-WILLIAMSTOWN 30-3-1912

SYSTEM CLOSED 1-2-34.

Tramway extension,Tynewydd
(Wyndham St.) to Blaenrhondda
(Brook St.), authorised 1915
but not built.

Trolley-bus route
to Gilfach Goch
(1914-15 only)

PORTH

Porth Depot
(not to scale)

RHONDDA TRAMWAYS

Rhondda Tramways Co. No. 50 in original 1908 open-top condition at Tonypandy.
(Courtesy A. D. Packer

The same car (50) at Tylorstown on the Maerdy route after being fitted with a top cover.
(M. Brookes

East Rd. Tylorstown

Rhondda Tramways 24 waiting for a crew-change outside Porth depot in 1930.
(Dr. H. A. Whitcombe courtesy Science Museum

24

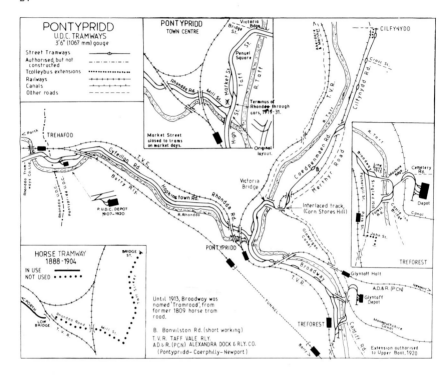

The opening ceremony of Pontypridd's electric tramways on 6 March 1905, with three cars of series 7-12 about to start from the Council Offices. *(Pontypridd Library*

PONTYPRIDD

Pontypridd 7 at Penuel Square, about 1920. By this time, cars 7-12 had been rebuilt with extended canopies.
(Commercial postcard

Pontypridd Council's main tram depot at Treforest on the day of the official opening, 6 March 1905.
(Pontypridd Library

Pontypridd 21 at Cilfynydd terminus in early 1930. The trams were replaced by single-deck trolleybuses in September.
(Dr. H. A. Whitcombe courtesy Science Museum

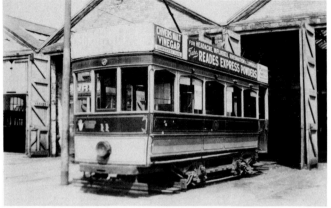

**ABERDARE
IN 1930**

**Aberdare 11 of
1913 outside the
depot at Gadlys.**
*(Dr. H. A. Whitcombe
courtesy Science
Museum*

**Aberdare 9 of
1914 at Lewis
Street, Aberaman,
bound for Aber-
cwmboi.**
*(Dr. H. A. Whitcombe
courtesy Science
Museum*

**Aberdare 25 of
1921 passing
Gadlys School en
route for
Trecynon.**
*(Dr. H. A. Whitcombe
courtesy Science
Museum*

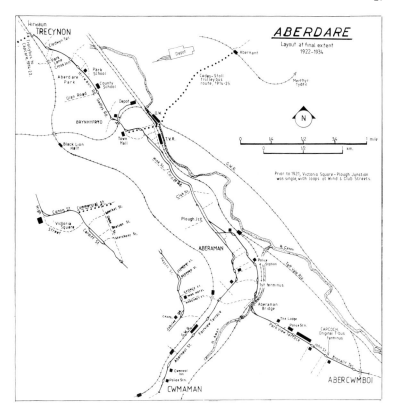

ABERDARE
Layout at final extent
1922-1934

Prior to 1921, Victoria Square-Plough Junction
was single, with loops at Wind & Club Streets.

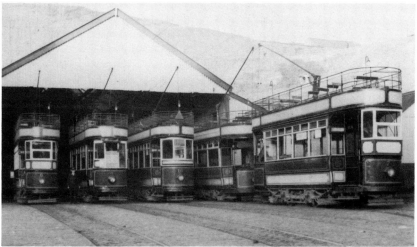

Merthyr 8, 6, 13, 10 and 7 at the depot at Penydaren in July 1938. All except No. 10 were secondhand (see the fleet list on page 45). *(W. A. Camwell*

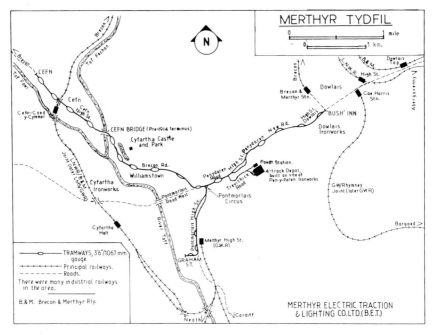

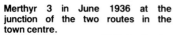

Merthyr 3 in June 1936 at the
junction of the two routes in the
town centre.

(G. N. Southerden

Merthyr 10 passing the Theatre Royal,
driven by a member of the engineering
staff. This car was latterly used as the
works car.   (G. N. Southerden

MERTHYR TYDFIL

One of Merthyr's original single-deck cars at Dowlais terminus. Eleven of these cars were later rebuilt as double-deckers. *(TMS*

Merthyr trams 6 and 13 in Brecon Road on the Cefn Coed route, 8 April 1939. The entire Merthyr system was single-track-and-loop, mainly in narrow roads; it closed on 23 August 1939.
(H. B. Priestley

A top-deck view of Merthyr tram No. 9 at Cefn Coed terminus on 29 May 1939.
(J. C. Gillham

NEATH

Neath Corporation gas-engined tram No. 19 at Briton Ferry terminus. This car came from Lytham St. Annes in 1903.
(TMS

No. 20 and one of the original small cars in Neath's depot at the time operation ceased in 1920.　*(TMS*

The surviving Neath gas tram in 1989, during restoration in the Neath Youth Community Training Workshop.
(J. H. Price

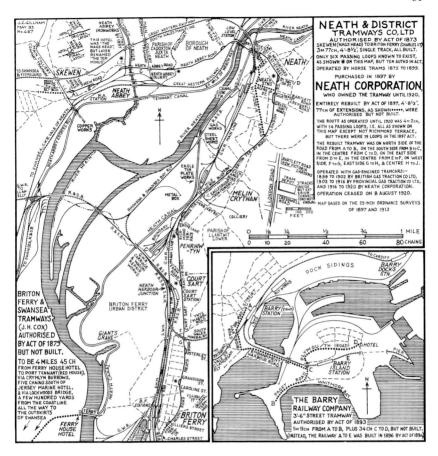

J.C.GILLHAM
MAY 93
No.467

NEATH & DISTRICT
TRAMWAYS CO,LTD
AUTHORISED BY ACT OF 1873
SKEWEN (NAGS HEAD) TO BRITON FERRY (CHARLES ST)
3M 77CH, 4'-8½', SINGLE TRACK, ALL BUILT.
ONLY SIX PASSING LOOPS KNOWN TO EXIST,
AS SHOWN ✱ ON THIS MAP, BUT TEN AUTHD IN ACT.
OPERATED BY HORSE TRAMS 1875 TO 1899.

PURCHASED IN 1897 BY
NEATH CORPORATION,
WHO OWNED THE TRAMWAY UNTIL 1920.

ENTIRELY REBUILT BY ACT OF 1897, 4'-8½'.
77CH OF EXTENSIONS, AS SHOWN •••••, WERE
AUTHORISED BUT NOT BUILT.

THE ROUTE AS OPERATED UNTIL 1920 WAS 4M 2CH,
WITH 14 PASSING LOOPS, I.E. ALL AS SHOWN ON
THIS MAP EXCEPT NOT RICHMOND TERRACE,
BUT THERE WERE 19 LOOPS IN THE 1897 ACT.

THE REBUILT TRAMWAY WAS ON NORTH SIDE OF THE
ROAD FROM A TO B, ON THE SOUTH SIDE FROM B TO C,
IN THE CENTRE FROM C TO D, ON THE EAST SIDE
FROM D TO E, IN THE CENTRE FROM E TO F, ON WEST
SIDE F TO G, EAST SIDE G TO H, & CENTRE H TO J.

OPERATED WITH GAS-ENGINED TRAMCARS:-
1899 TO 1902 BY BRITISH GAS TRACTION CO LTD,
1902 TO 1916 BY PROVINCIAL GAS TRACTION CO LTD,
AND 1916 TO 1920 BY NEATH CORPORATION.
OPERATION CEASED ON 8 AUGUST 1920.

MAP BASED ON THE 25-INCH ORDNANCE SURVEYS
OF 1897 AND 1913

BRITON
FERRY &
SWANSEA
TRAMWAYS
(J.H. COX)
AUTHORISED
BY ACT OF 1879
BUT NOT BUILT.

TO BE 4 MILES 45 CH
FROM FERRY HOUSE HOTEL
TO PORT TENNANT (RED HOUSE),
VIA CRYMLYN BURROWS,
FIVE CHAINS SOUTH OF
JERSEY MARINE HOTEL,
& VIA LOCKWOODS BRIDGE,
A FEW HUNDRED YARDS
FROM THE COASTLINE
ALL THE WAY TO
THE OUTSKIRTS
OF SWANSEA

THE BARRY
RAILWAY COMPANY.
3'-6" STREET TRAMWAY
AUTHORISED BY ACT OF 1893
1M 11CH FROM A TO B, PLUS 34 CH C TO D, BUT NOT BUILT.
(INSTEAD, THE RAILWAY A TO E WAS BUILT IN 1896 BY ACT OF 1894)

The Oystermouth Tramroad at Swansea was the world's first pas- senger railway (from March 1807). Until steam traction began in 1877, passengers travelled in horse- drawn open cars or in compartment carriages with ladders and roof sets.
(BET Gazette

THE MUMBLES

ANCIENT—
For the first seventy years horses were the motive power of the Swansea — Mumbles Railway

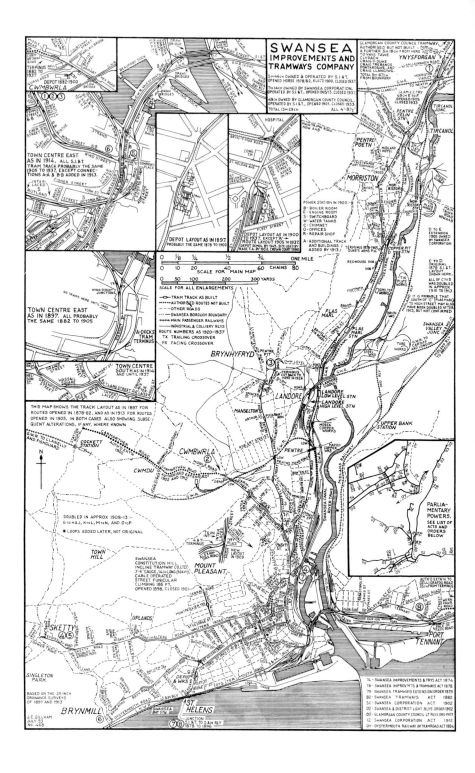

SWANSEA
IMPROVEMENTS AND TRAMWAYS COMPANY

SCALE FOR MAIN MAP — ONE MILE

Tram Track as built

J.C. GILLHAM
JULY 93
No. 468

SWANSEA

From 1898 to 1901, Swansea had a 3ft 6in gauge street funicular, the Swansea Constitution Hill Incline Tramway. It was not a success.
(Tramway and Railway World

At the Tramways Exhibition held in London in July 1900, the Brush Electrical Engineering Co. Ltd. exhibited a bogie car built for Swansea, No. 23 of Series 16-30.
(Courtesy M. J. O'Connor

Swansea's mystery tram, open-top No. 68, turning into Alexandra Road near the GWR station in 1911. It ran in Swansea, probably on hire, until replaced by a new bogie single-decker in 1914. The small single-decker on the right is one of Swansea 1-15.
(TMS

34

SWANSEA TRAMWAYS, JUNE 1936

Bogie car No. 43 at Sketty terminus.
(G. N. Southerden)

Brush lowbridge car No. 4 in High Street.
(G. N. Southerden)

Nos. 63 and 70 in Oxford Street, looking west.
(G. N. Southerden)

**SWANSEA,
JUNE 1936**

No. 18 in High
Street, a short dis-
tance south of the
GWR station.
(G. N. Southerden

No. 72 at Port
Tennant terminus
on service 8 to
Civic Centre (near
St. Helens depot).
(G. N. Southerden

No. 78 in High
Street, just north
of the GWR
station, en route
for Cwmbwrla.
(G. N. Southerden

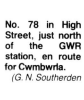

SWANSEA & MUMBLES

A well-known photograph of an Oystermouth Tramroad train in 1877, headed by a Hughes Patent tramway engine.
(Science Museum, Whitcombe Collection

Locomotive No. 1 (Black Hawthorn 1072/1892) at Southend about 1900 on a train comprising one closed workmen's car, one first class bogie car and four second class four-wheelers, one of which is a narrow ex-horse tram.
(J. H. Price collection

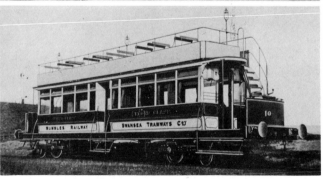

One of the two battery cars built by Brush in 1902 and tried in 1903. They were not a success and were soon converted to trailers for the steam service. One served as a royal special for a docks ceremony in 1904.
(Tramway and Railway World

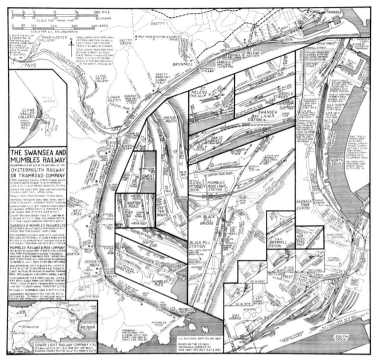

An enlargement of this map will be published in *Tramway Review* during 1994.

The arrival of a Swansea & Mumbles steam train at Mumbles Pier, about 1906, including four of the first class bogie trailers built by G. F. Milnes in 1893 and 1902. Second class passengers rode in four-wheel cars, some of which were former horse trams placed on wagon underframes. *(TMS*

SWANSEA & MUMBLES

Electric car No. 1 at Rutland St. depot in the original mainly-cream livery of 1928/9. This was changed to mainly dark red in about 1935/6.

(G. N. Southerden

At busy times the 106-seat electric cars ran in multiple-unit pairs. This train is leaving Southend for Mumbles Pier; the date is 4 August 1948.

(Ian L. Wright

No. 3 at Mumbles Pier terminus on 28 September 1952, showing the pantograph current collector.

(W. J. Wyse

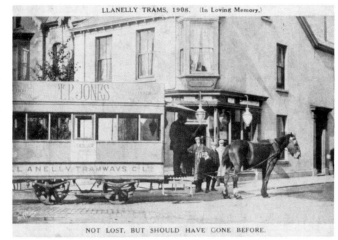

LLANELLY TRAMS, 1908. (In Loving Memory.)

NOT LOST, BUT SHOULD HAVE GONE BEFORE.

LLANELLY

Llanelly bade fare-well to its 3ft gauge horse trams in April 1908, but the service re-started on standard-gauge track and ran until electric services began in July 1911.
(Commercial postcard

Two of Llanelly's 16 electric trams at the GWR station terminus.
(Dr. Hugh Nicol

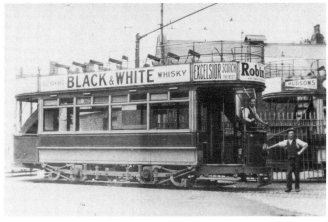

Llanelly 13 at the depot in 1930. The different batches of Llanelly trams could be distinguished by their truck types.
(Dr. H. A. Whitcombe courtesy Science Museum

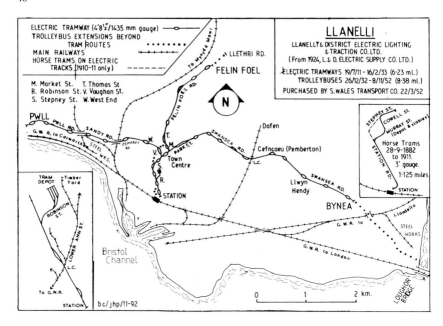

Tramcar Fleet Lists

All cars were four-wheel double-deck unless otherwise stated.
Seating figures shown thus: 22/34 are for lower and upper decks respectively.
The opening dates shown are the first day of regular public service.
The closing dates shown are the last full day of public service.

Aberdare Urban District Council Tramways

5.77 miles, 3ft 6in gauge, opened 9 October 1913, closed 31 March 1935. Livery: maroon and white.

Car Numbers	Type (as built)	Year Built	Builder	Seats	Truck(s)	Motors	Controllers
1-5, 10	Open top	1921	Brush	22/26	Peckham P22	MV 323V 2 x 35 hp	MV TI/C
6-9	Open top	1914	Brush	22/26	Peckham P22	Westinghouse 200 DK DBI K4 2 x 35 hp	
11-20	Single Deck	1913	Brush	26	Peckham P22	Westinghouse 200 DK DB1 K4 2 x 30 hp	
21-26	Open top	1921	Brush	22/26	Peckham P22	MV 323V 2 x 35 hp	MV TI/C

Aberdare UDC also operated trolleybuses from 15 January 1914 to 23 July 1925.

Cardiff Tramways Co. Ltd.

6.31 miles, horse traction, 4ft 8½in gauge, opened 12 July 1872, purchased by Cardiff Corporation 1 January 1902, replaced by electric trams by 17 October 1902. Maximum 52 cars. Four cars sold to Guernsey for use as trailers, one preserved in Cardiff.

Cardiff District and Penarth Harbour Tramway Co. Ltd.

2.41 miles, horse traction, 4ft 8½in gauge, opened 28 November 1881, operated by S. Andrews to 1887, by Provincial Tramways from 1 April 1888 until Corporation purchase and electrification in 1903. 11 cars built 1881 by S. Andrews, replaced by new Brush cars post-1888.

Cardiff Corporation Tramways

19.51 miles (at maximum), 4ft 8½in gauge, opened 2 May 1902, closed 19 February 1950 (closing ceremony on 20 February). Livery: crimson lake and cream (some cars grey from 1942). The trams were replaced by trolleybuses which operated from 1 March 1942 to 11 January 1970.

Car Numbers	Type (as built)	Year Built	Builder	Seats	Truck(s)	Motors	Controllers
1-20 (note a)	Open top uncanopied	1902	ER&TCW	22/30	Brill 21E	DK 25A 2 x 25 hp	DK DB1 Form B
21-40 (note b)	Open top uncanopied	1902	ER&TCW	30/38 (note b)	Brill 22E MxT bogies	DK 25A 2 x 25 hp(b)	DK DB1 Form B (note b)
41-54 (note h)	Single deck	1902	ER&TCW	34	Brill 22E MxT bogies	DK 25A 2 x 25 hp	DK DB1 Form B
55-74 (note a)	Open top uncanopied	1902	ER&TCW	22/30	Brill 21E	DK 25A 2 x 25 hp	DK DB1 Form B
75-94 (note b)	Open top uncanopied	1902	ER&TCW	30/38 (note b)	Brill 22E MxT bogies	DK 25A 2 x 25 hp	DK DB1 Form B
95-114 (note a)	Open top uncanopied	1903	Brush	22/30	Brill 21E	GE58-6T 2 x 28 hp	BTH B18
115 (note c)	Single deck combination	1903	Milnes	36	Brill 22E MxT bogies	GE58-6T 2 x 28 hp	BTH B18 (note c)
116-130 (note c)	Single deck combination	1904	Milnes	40	Brush MxT bogies	GE58-6T 2 x 28 hp	BTH B18
131 (note d)	Water car/ Sweeper	1902	ER&TCW	—	Brill 21E	DK 25A 2 x 25 hp	DK DB1 Form B
101 (II)	Enclosed lowbridge	1923	Brush	24/40	Peckham P22	GE 265 2 x 40 hp	BTH B510A
25 cars (note e)	Enclosed lowbridge	1923/4	Brush	24/40	Peckham P22	BTH 265A 2 x 40 hp	BTH B510A
55 cars (note f)	Enclosed lowbridge	1924/5	Brush	24/40	Peckham P22	BTH 265A 2 x 40 hp	BTH B510E
53 (II) (note g)	Single deck	1926	Brush	44	Peckham P25 MxT bogies	BTH 506A 2 x 40 hp	BTH B510E
30 cars (note g)	Single deck	1927	Brush	44	Peckham P25 MxT bogies	BTH 506A 2 x 40 hp	BTH B510E

Notes

(a) Car 3 used as parcels and ticket car 1903-20. Cars 5, 6, 10, 13, 72, 99 rebuilt c.1922 with canopies, drivers' windscreens and Peckham P22 trucks (seating 22/38). Four cars renumbered post-1926 as 138-141 (138 ex 3, 139 ex 7, 140 ex 19, 141 ex 98).

(b) Cars 22, 23, 24, 29,30, 32, 34, 76, 84, 90 rebuilt with canopies and drivers' windscreens in 1922 (24 in 1921), seating 30/48, with GE 200K 40 hp motors and BTH B49 controllers. Car 30 had these from 1914.

(c) Cars 115 and 125 received drivers' windscreens; GE 200K 40 hp motors and BTH B510 controllers in 1923. Cars 116/7 received B510 controllers and one later became 146.

(d) Un-numbered 1902-5 and 1926-49. Hurst Nelson track shoes fitted 1920. Preserved by TMS from 1950.

(e) Nos. 2, 9, 20, 56, 57, 62, 66, 70, 95, 96, 97, 100, 102-114.

(f) Nos. 1, 3, 4, 7, 8, 11, 14, 16-19, 21, 25-28, 31, 33, 35-40, 55, 58-60, 63-65, 67-69, 71, 73-75, 77-83, 85-89, 91-94, 98.

(g) Nos. 41, 44, 46, 47, 49-54, 116-124, 126-137. These cars were sold in 1940 to Para (Brazil) and ran there until 1947.

(h) One car of this series became 144 c. 1926. One car of series 21-40 became 142. Numbers 143/5 not used.

Llanelly Tramways Company Ltd.

0.97 miles, horse traction, 3ft 0in gauge, 5 single deck cars, opened 28 September 1882. Closed for conversion to standard gauge 31 March 1908; reopened with three double deck cars (ex-London), replaced by electric trams 19 July 1911.

Llanelly and District Electric Supply Co. Ltd. (see text for earlier titles).

6.23 miles, opened 19 July 1911, closed 16 February 1933. Livery: green and ivory. The trams were replaced by trolleybuses, which operated from 26 December 1932 to 8 November 1952, (owned by SWT from 22 March 1952).

Car Numbers	Type (as built)	Year Built	Builder	Seats	Truck(s)	Motors	Controllers
1-10	Open top	1911	UEC	24/40	Brill 21E	GE 58-4T 2 x 37½ hp	BTH GE K 10-D
11-14	Open top	1912	UEC	24/40	Peckham P22	GE 58-4T 2 x 37½ hp	BTH GE K 10-D
15-16	Open top	1920	EE	24/40	Peckham P22	GE 200K 2 x 40 hp	BTH (secondhand?)

Two cars were acquired from Mansfield 1918, but were subsequently returned (probably in 1920).

42

Merthyr Electric Traction & Lighting Co. Ltd.

3.50 miles, 3ft 6in gauge, opened 6 April 1901, closed 23 August 1939. Livery: bright green and ivory (originally dark red and ivory?).

Car Numbers	Type (as built)	Year Built	Builder	Seats	Truck(s)	Motors (b)	Controllers
1-13	Single deck (note a)	1900	Midland	26	Brill 21E	GE 58-4T 2 x 37 hp	GE K10D
14-16	Open top	1901	ER&TCW	48	Brill 21E	Walker 33N 2 x 25 hp	DK DE1 Form B
10 (II)	Open top	1909	Brush	45	Brill 21E	GE 58-4T 2 x 37 hp	GE K10D
9 cars (note c)	Open top	(bought 1929/30)	B&MTJC	22/26	Brill 21E	GE 58-4T 2 x 37 hp	GE K10D
3, 4, 6, 12 (II) (d)	Open top	(bought 1933)	UEC	22/26	Brill 21E	DK 6A(d) 2 x 35 hp	DK DB1 Form G1 (note d)

Notes

(a) No. 10 withdrawn after accident in 1903, truck and equipment to No. 10 (II). Nos. 2-4, 6-9 and 11-13 rebuilt as 45-seat open top cars between 1910 and 1915.
(b) One car re-equipped 1923 with BTH 249AA motors (2 x 37 hp).
(c) Nos. 2, 7, 8, 9, 11, 13, 14, 15, 16 (II). Bodies (built at Tividale) bought from Birmingham & Midland Tramways Joint Committee 1929/30 (built 1913-16) and remounted on trucks from original Merthyr cars.
(d) Bought 1933 from Birmingham Corporation with equipment shown, replaced on cars 3, 4, 6 at Merthyr with GE equipment from 1900/1 cars. Built 1905-8, Merthyr 12 was Birmingham 226, others not known.

Newport Tramways Company

1.5 miles, 4ft 8½in gauge, horse traction, opened 1 February 1875, leased to E. Perry 1881-5, operation ceased 28 July 1894. Cars 1-5 16-seat single deck by Starbuck 1875, 1892 stock 8 double deck knifeboard seat.

Newport Corporation Tramways (pre-electric)

3.3 miles (5 miles from 1899), 4ft 8½in gauge, horse traction, reopened 30 July 1894, leased to Solomon Andrews to 29 July 1901, horse operation ceased 3 November 1903. Maximum 26 cars (new and secondhand). Livery: green and cream.

Newport Corporation Tramways

8.55 miles, 4ft 8½in gauge, opened 9 April 1903, closed 5 September 1937. Livery: cherry red and cream (maroon and cream from 1920). Some cars wartime grey.

Car Numbers	Type (as built)	Year Built	Builder	Seats	Truck(s)	Motors	Controllers
1-30	Open top (note a)	1902/3	Milnes	22/33	Peckham Cantilever	Westinghouse 2 x 30 hp	Westinghouse 90
31-40 (note b)	Open top	1904	ER&TCW	22/33	Brill 21E	DK 25A 2 x 25 hp	DK DB1 Form E
41	Water car/ grinder	1906	UEC	—	Brill 21E	DK 3A4 2 x 35 hp	DK DB Form E
42-44	Open top	1909	UEC	22/23	Brill 21E	DK 3A 2 x 35 hp	DK DB1 Form E
45-50 (note c)	Enclosed top	Bought 1917 (note c)	ER&TCW	22/34	Brill 21E	DK 25A 2 x 25 hp	DK DB1 Form D
51-54	Enclosed top bogie	1921	Brush	80	Preston 22E M&T bogies	DK 30B 2 x 40 hp	DK DB1 K3
55-58	Enclosed top	1922	Hurst Nelson	55	Preston 21E	DK 29A 2 x 30 hp	DK DB1 K3

Notes

(a) Cars 1-30 were reconstructed by Newport between 1912 and 1916 (No. 22 by Brush in 1923). 22, 29 and 30 received Westinghouse 90M controllers and magnetic track brakes in 1907. Car 16 received a Hurst Nelson 21E truck in 1921.
(b) Car 31 was fitted with a Hurst Nelson truck and Westinghouse equipment in 1924. Car 34 was rebuilt all-enclosed in 1928, with MV OK6B controllers.
(c) Cars 45-50 were built for the LCC in 1903 (Class B). The six cars for Newport were chosen from LCC 105, 114, 115, 127, 136, 137, 142, 146, 159 and 164.

Neath and District Tramways Company

3.96 miles, 4ft 8½in gauge, horse traction, opened 19 November 1875, 8 cars purchased by Neath Corporation 7 August 1896, replaced by gas trams in 1899.

Neath Corporation Tramways

4.02 miles, 4ft 8½in gauge, worked by gas-engined cars 31 August 1899 to 8 August 1920. Leased to British Gas Traction Co. Ltd. 1899-1902, leased to Provincial Gas Traction Co. Ltd. 1902-1916, operated by Neath Corporation 1916-1920. 4 cars built new, 1899; remainder transferred from Lytham, 1903. Small cars (including 1-3) built by Ashbury Railway Carriage & Iron Co. Ltd. (seats 16/24); large cars (including 18-23) built by Lancaster Railway Carriage and Wagon Co. Ltd. (seats 22/30). Replaced by motor buses of South Wales Transport Co. Ltd. 9 August 1920. One of the small cars has been preserved locally. Livery: chocolate and cream (preserved car is green).

Pontypridd and Rhondda Valley Tramway Company

3.03 miles, 3ft 6in gauge, horse traction, opened March 1888 with eight double deck cars, purchased by BET 1 March 1899, 14 cars in 1900, sold to local councils and operations ceased July 1903.

Pontypridd Urban District Council Tramways

5.34 miles, 3ft 6in gauge, opened 5 March 1905, closed 30 August 1931. Livery: maroon and cream.

Car Numbers	Type (as built)	Year Built	Builder	Seats	Truck(s)	Motors	Controllers
1-6	Single deck combination	1904	Brush	28	Brill 22E bogies	GE 58-4T 2 x 37 hp	BTH B18
7-12	Open top uncanopied	1904	Brush	46	Brill 22E bogies	GE 58-4T 2 x 37 hp	BTH B18
13-20	Open top	1907	Brush	54	M&G Type 4 bogies	GE 58-4T 2 x 37 hp	BTH B18
21-26	Open top	1908	UEC	54	M&G Type 4 bogies	GE 58-4T 2 x 37 hp	BTH B18
27-31	Short top cover	1920	Brush	54	Brill 22E bogies	GE 249 2 x 37 hp	BTH B18

Cars 7-12 were given extended canopies in 1914 (54 seats) and received short top covers in 1921-3.
Cars 13-26 received UEC short top covers between 1910 and 1914.
Car 4 used as permanent way car. Car 2 used as snowplough.
The trams were partly replaced by trolleybuses, which ran from 18 September 1930 to 31 January 1957.

Rhondda Tramways Co. Ltd.

20.92 miles, 3ft 6in gauge, opened 11 July 1908, closed 1 February 1934. Livery: maroon and yellow.

Car Numbers	Type (as built)	Year Built	Builder	Seats	Truck(s)	Motors	Controllers
1-50	Open top	1908	Brush	22/26	Brush AA	GE 58-4T 2 x 37 hp	BTH B18
51-54	Balcony	1913	Brush	22/26	Brush AA	GE 58-4T 2 x 37 hp	BTH B18

Cars 3, 7-13, 16, 18, 20, 21, 24, 30, 32-35, 39-42, 44, 45 and 47-50 were given open balcony top covers between 1909 and 1913, plus a short top cover on No. 5. Further cars were top-covered in 1923-28. A trolleybus service was operated from 22 December 1914 to March 1915 (vehicles sold 1920 to Teesside).

Swansea Improvements and Tramways Company Limited

5.49 miles, 4ft 8½in gauge, horse traction, opened 12 April 1878, 25 cars. Steam traction with two Hughes engines on Cwmbwrla route in 1882-84. Electric traction commenced 30 June 1900, 13.36 miles (including 7.18 miles leased from Swansea Corporation), closed 29 June 1937. Livery: maroon and cream.

Car Numbers	Type (as built)	Year Built	Builder	Seats	Truck(s)	Motors	Controllers
1-15	Single deck (note a)	1900	Brush	26	Baltimore	Brush 800A 2 x 17 hp	Brush H2 (note b)
16-30	Single deck	1900	Brush	44	Baltimore MxT bogies	Brush 1000A 2 x 25 hp	Brush (note b)
31-41	Open top (note c)	1899 (note c)	Brush	22/32	Peckham Cantilever	GE 52-6T 2 x 20 hp	GE K10
42-45	Open top (note d)	Bought 1904	ER&TCW	32/36	Brill 22E MxT bogies	DK 35A 2 x 35 hp	DK DB1 Form B
46-49	Open top (note e)	Bought 1904	Brush	22/28	Brill 21E	GE 52-6T 2 x 20 hp	BTH B18

Notes
(a) Cars 1 and 2 used as works cars from c.1920.
(b) Replaced at various dates by Westinghouse TI/C controllers.
(c) Built for Leeds, resold to Swansea by BTH in 1899 with new BTH/GE equipment. Entered service as single deck, stairs and top seats fitted late 1900, balcony top covers by UEC and SI&T 1907/8.
(d) Built for Gravesend 1902 (Gravesend 7?, 8?, 9, 10).
(e) Built for Weston-super-Mare 1902 (Weston series 1-8). Balcony top covers by UEC 1913.

Swansea Improvements and Tramways Company Limited (continued)

Car Numbers	Type (as built)	Year Built	Builder	Seats	Truck(s)	Motors	Controllers
50-55	Single deck combination (note f)	Bought 1905 (note f)	ER&TCW	42	Brill 22E MxT bogies	Brush (note f)	Brush (note f)
56-61	Single deck combination	1906	Brush	44	Brush MxT bogies	Brush 1002B 2 x 25 hp	Brush (note b)
62-65	Open top	1906	Brush	24/32	Brush Conaty (g)	Brush 1002B 2 x 25 hp	Brush (note b)
66	Single deck combination	1911	Brush	46	Brush MET MxT bogies	Westinghouse 2 x 42 hp	Westinghouse TI/C
67	Single deck combination	1911	SI&T	42	Brush MET MxT bogies	Westinghouse 2 x 42 hp	Westinghouse TI/C
68	Open top	(hired 1911-14)	Brush	?	Brush AA	Brush or Westinghouse	Brush or Westinghouse
69-74	Single deck	1912/3	Brush	46	Brush MET MxT bogies	Westinghouse 2 x 42 hp	Westinghouse TI/C
68 (II)	Single deck	1914	Brush	42	Brush MET MxT bogies	Westinghouse 2 x 42 hp	Westinghouse TI/C
75-79	Single deck	1921	Brush	44	Brush MET MxT bogies	BTH GE264 2 x 32½ hp	BTH B18

Replacement and Rebuilt cars

Car Numbers	Type (as built)	Year Built	Builder	Seats	Truck(s)	Motors	Controllers
20, 51 (note k)	Single deck	1912	SI&T	42	Baltimore MxT bogies	Westinghouse 2 x 42 hp	Westinghouse TI/C
50, 52 (note k)	Single deck	1913	SI&T	42	SI&T MxT bogies	Westinghouse 2 x 42 hp	Westinghouse TI/C
21 (note j)	Single deck	1915	SI&T	42	Baltimore MxT bogies	Westinghouse 2 x 42 hp	Westinghouse TI/C
18, 19 (note j)	Single deck	1916	SI&T	42	SI&T MxT bogies	Westinghouse 2 x 42 hp	Westinghouse TI/C
53, 54 (note k)	Single deck	1919	SI&T	42	SI&T MxT bogies (note h)	Westinghouse 2 x 42 hp	Westinghouse TI/C
16, 17 (note j)	Single deck	1921	SI&T	46	SI&T MxT bogies	Westinghouse 2 x 42 hp	Westinghouse TI/C
33-41 (note a)	Balcony	Rebuilt 1920	Brush/ SI&T	22/32	Peckham Cantilever	?	Westinghouse TI/C
56-61	Single deck	Rebuilt 1921	Brush/ SI&T	40	Brush MxT bogies	GE 200K 2 x 40 hp	BTH B18
46-49	Enclosed top	Rebuilt 1922	Brush/ SI&T	22/26	Brill 21E	?	BTH B18
5-15	Enclosed lowbridge	1923	Brush	24/38	Peckham P22	BTH 265A 2 x 40 hp	BTH B510
62-65	Enclosed	Rebuilt 1924	Brush/ SI&T	24/40	SI&T 4 wheel	?	BTH B18
42-45	Enclosed	Rebuilt 1924	SI&T	34/52	SI&T MxT bogies	BTH 509CH 2 x 50 hp (1926)	BTH B18 (note c)
3, 4	Enclosed lowbridge	1925	Brush	24/38	Peckham P22	BTH 265A 2 x 40 hp	BTH B510
22-35	Enclosed lowbridge	(note e)	SI&T	24/40	SI&T 4-wheel	(note n)	(note d)

Notes
(a) Car 40 (ex 33) enclosed top.
(b) Replaced at various dates by Westinghouse controllers.
(c) Controllers fitted with BTH line breakers, 1927.
(d) Controllers in 1936: 24 EE DB1 K3, 25-28 and 31-35 BTH B18, 29-30 BTH B510, 22-23 BTH B18 with line-breaker.
(e) Built 1926 (29, 30), 1927 (27, 28), 1928 (25, 26), 1929 (31-33), 1931 (22-24), 1933 (34, 35). One of these cars (23?) was originally numbered 21.
(f) Built 1901 for Middleton Electric Traction Co. Ltd. Sold to Swansea without equipment.
(g) One car retrucked with M&G Warner Radial truck 1908. All received SI&T single trucks in 1924.
(h) Baltimore maximum-traction bogies in car 54.
(j) These cars were numbered 22-24, 26 and 28 when first rebuilt (order not known).
(k) One car in series 20 and 50-54 thought to have exchanged numbers with 66.
(n) 8 cars BTH 265A, 6 cars BTH 509A 12 (50 hp).

General note: Motors and controllers were frequently exchanged for other types during overhauls. Full details not available.

Swansea and Mumbles Railway (1929-60)

5.38 miles, 4ft 8½in gauge. Electric operation began 2 March 1929, line closed 5 January 1960. (Southend to Mumbles closed 12 October 1959).

Car Numbers	Type (as built)	Year Built	Builder	Seats	Truck(s)	Motors	Controllers
1-11	Enclosed double deck	1928	Brush	48/58	Brush equal wheel bogies	BTH 509BH 2 x 60 hp	BTH C613A contactor control
12-13	Enclosed double deck	1929	Brush	48/58	Brush equal wheel bogies	BTH 509BH 2 x 60 hp	BTH C613A contactor control

Non-powered auxiliary vehicles; tower wagon 16, ballast wagon 17, weedkiller tank 18.

Swansea and Mumbles Railway — rolling stock summary, 1883 to 1927

Date	Steam Loco-motives	Double deck cars	D/deck summer cars	(Converted) battery cars	Workmen's closed cars	Open excursion cars	Total trailer cars
1883	3	?	–	–	2	?	25
Oct. 1896	5	16	–	–	2	6	24
Oct. 1900	5	18	–	–	2	14	34
Oct. 1902	5	18	4	2	2	14	40
Jan. 1905	5	18	4	(2)	2	13	39
June 1906	5	19	4	(2)	2	13	40
June 1912	5	19	4	(2)	2	13	40
1918	4	19	4	(2)	2	13	40
1923	4	19?	4	(2)	2	12?	39
1927	4	19?	4	(2)	2	12?	39

5.38 miles, 4ft 8½in gauge, horse traction, passenger service commenced 25 March 1807, ceased 1828, (?), resumed 1860, mixed steam and horse traction 1877-1896, then steam-only to 1929. Extension from Oystermouth to Mumbles Pier opened 10 May 1898.

Swansea and Mumbles trailer cars

1807 stock was one passenger vehicle ("Llewellyn's Coach"). 1860 stock comprised two compartment carriages with roof seats and two open toastracks, all withdrawn about 1883. Tramway type single-sided vehicles introduced 1877. Livery: originally brown, from 1893 first class cars crimson lake and cream, second class cars brown or brown and cream. Stock is shown as in 1904; not all cars were externally numbered.

Car Numbers	Type	Class	Year Built	Builder	Running Gear	Seats
1-4 (a)	Double deck garden seat	First	1893	Milnes	bogies	32/46?
5-8 (a)	Double deck crossbench garden seat	First	1902	Milnes (Hadley)	MxT bogies (note b)	48/52? (note h)
9-10 (c)	Double deck ex-battery centre door	First	1902	Brush	Brush bogies	42/57
11-17 (d)	Double deck knifeboard top seat	Second	1877/8, 1885	Starbuck & Falcon	4-wheel	24/24
18-19 (e)	Double deck garden seat	Second	1891	Milnes	4-wheel	?
One car	Double deck ex-horse (f)	Second	(rebuilt 1903)	S&M ex Starbuck	4-wheel	?
4 cars (g)	Double deck ex-horse	Second	(Before 1891)	?	4-wheel	?
2 cars	Single deck Workmen's	Workmen	c.1883	SWC	4-wheel	60
14 cars	Open cars, bench seats	Excursion	1880s	SWC	4-wheel	60

Notes

(a) Number groups possibly reversed (1-4 1902, 5-8 1893).
(b) Designed for conversion to electric cars.
(c) Batteries and Brush motors and controllers removed winter 1903/4.
(d) Original Starbuck cars of 1877/8 and similar cars built by Falcon in 1885, given railway underframes, with buffers and couplings, by 1896.
(e) Originally first class. Brakesman's cabin on one platform.
(f) Rebuilt by S&M on long underframe with verandah.

(g) Original narrow horse cars used for SI&T/SM through service to 1896 (original 7-10?). Remounted 1896/7 on railway underframes with buffers and couplings.
(h) Seats 60/48 if seating five-abreast on lower deck.
1925 traffic totals: 628,108 passengers (140,814 first class, 278,528 second class, 14,804 excursion, 247,962 workmen), 8994 tons of freight.

Swansea and Mumbles Railway — Locomotives owned

Stock Number	Type	Year Built	Year Bought	Builder	Works Number	Name	Withdrawn
1	0-4-0 Tram	1877	1877	Hughes	8	Pioneer	1884(b)
2	0-4-0 Tram	1877	1877	Hughes	9	Progress	1886(a)
3	0-4-0 Tram	1877	1877	Hughes	10	Alexandra	1888(a)
3	0-4-0 ST*	1879	1886	Manning Wardle	712	—	1906
4	0-4-0 ST*	1879	1886	Manning Wardle	722	—	1898
5(c)	0-6-0T	1881	1886	Hunslet	265	—	1906
1	0-4-0ST*	1892	1892	Black Hawthorn	1072	—	(by 1918)
2	0-4-0ST*	1892	1892	Black Hawthorn	1073	—	(by 1918)
4	0-6-0T	1899	1899	Hunslet	697	—	1929(d)
5	0-6-0T	1899	1899	Hunslet	698	—	1929(d)
3	0-4-0ST	1906	1906	Brush	316	—	1929(d)
1	0-6-0ST	1906	1920	Avonside	1506	Swansea	1929(d)
14	4-whl petrol	1929	1929	Hardy	—	—	1954(e)
15	0-4-0DM	1936	1936	J. Fowler	21202	—	1960

Notes
* built with enclosed wheels and motion.
(a) Used on Swansea — Cwmbwrla tram route 1882-4, scrapped 1894.
(b) Returned to makers 1878 in exchange for Hughes 0-4-0ST (on loan?).
(c) Renumbered 3 in May 1899.
(d) One steam locomotive retained or hired until 1933-35.
(e) Parts used 1954 to build replica 1807 carriage.
Various other locomotives were operated on hire, mainly in 1923-29.
From 1878 to 1885 the railway was worked by lessees with their own locomotives.

Key to Abbreviations and Manufacturers

Avonside	—	The Avonside Co, Bristol.
Baltimore	—	The Baltimore Car Wheel and Truck Co, USA.
BET	—	The British Electric Traction Co Ltd.
B&MTJC	—	Birmingham and Midland Tramways Joint Committee, Tividale Works.
Brill	—	The J. G. Brill Company, Philadelphia, USA.
BTH	—	The British Thomson-Houston Co Ltd, Rugby.
Brush	—	The Brush Electrical Engineering Co Ltd, Loughborough.
DK	—	Dick, Kerr & Co Ltd, Preston.
EE	—	The English Electric Co Ltd, Preston.
ER&TCW	—	The Electric Railway & Tramway Carriage Works Limited, Preston.
Falcon	—	The Falcon Engine & Car Works, Loughborough.
Fowler	—	John Fowler & Co (Leeds) Ltd.
GE	—	The General Electric Co, Schenectady, USA.
GWR	—	Great Western Railway.
Hardy	—	Hardy Rail Motors Ltd, Slough.
Hughes	—	Henry Hughes & Co, Loughborough.
Hunslet	—	The Hunslet Engine Co Ltd, Hunslet, Leeds.
Hurst Nelson	—	Hurst Nelson & Co Ltd, Motherwell, Scotland.
LCC	—	London County Council.
LMSR	—	London Midland & Scottish Railway.
MET	—	Metropolitan Electric Tramways.
Midland	—	Midland Railway Carriage & Wagon Co Ltd, Shrewsbury.
Milnes	—	Geo. F. Milnes & Co Ltd, Birkenhead and Hadley.
M & G	—	Mountain and Gibson Ltd, Bury, Lancashire.
MxT	—	Maximum-traction.
MV	—	Metropolitan-Vickers Electrical Co Ltd, Trafford Park, Manchester.
MR&P	—	Mumbles Railway & Pier.
Peckham	—	Trucks built by or for the Peckham Truck & Engineering Co Ltd.
S&M	—	Swansea & Mumbles Railway.
SI&T	—	Swansea Improvements & Tramways Co Ltd.
Starbuck	—	George Starbuck & Company, Birkenhead.
SWC	—	The Swansea Wagon Co., Ltd.
TMS	—	The Tramway Museum Society, (Library of the National Tramway Museum, Crich, Derbyshire).
T&RW	—	*The Tramway and Railway World.*
UEC	—	United Electric Car Co Ltd, Preston.
Walker	—	The Walker Electric Company, Cleveland, USA.
Westinghouse	—	Westinghouse Electric Co Ltd, Trafford Park, Manchester.

THREE SURVIVORS

Lowbridge horse car 21 of the Cardiff Tramways Company Ltd. at the Welsh Industrial and Maritime Museum at Cardiff Pier Head. This car spent 65 years as a tea bar in Cardiff Docks.

(Welsh Industrial and Maritime Museum

Swansea Tramways 14 (actually 14's lower deck with No. 12's top) in Swansea Maritime and Industrial Museum, on a Bruxelles truck. These cars were built by Brush to pass under 15ft 0in railway bridges; Swansea had 13 such cars (Nos. 3-15) and Cardiff had 81. No. 14 was rebuilt as a Job Training programme after 40 years on a farm.

(Swansea Maritime and Industrial Museum

RUTLAND ST.
ST. HELENS
BRYNMILL
ASHLEIGH RD.
BLACKPILL
WEST CROSS
NORTON RD.
OYSTERMOUTH
SOUTHEND
MUMBLES PIER

Cardiff's water tram 131 at the British Flottman works in 1951. It arrived at Crich Tramway Museum in May 1959.

Ian L. Wright

Acknowledgments and Sources

This book is based on Chapter 8 of *Great British Tramway Networks* by W. H. Bett and J. C. Gillham (LRTL, 1962), revised in the light of new research and recent books and articles. Foremost among these were the articles by H. B. Priestley in *Tramway Review* on the tramways of Cardiff and Swansea, and other helpers include D. Beynon, C. Taylor, P. Trotter, N. Wassell and R. J. S. Wiseman. A. A. Jackson and P. Trotter supplied many entries for the Bibliography. The fleet lists on page 40 to 46 have presented greater difficulties than in any previous books in this series, and certain points in regard to Swansea tramways and the pre-electric Swansea and Mumbles Railway are still unresolved. The lists have been compiled by J. H. Price, with the valued assistance of G. E. Baddeley, D. Beynon, G. Gabb, F. P. Groves, E. R. Oakley, H. B. Priestley and P. Trotter. The publishers will be pleased to receive any additional information from readers, and this will be published in *Tramway Review*.

The maps of Neath, Newport and Swansea and the general map of South Wales have been drawn by J. C. Gillham, and the map of Cardiff by David Gould, from his book *Cardiff's Electric Tramways* (Oakwood Press, 1974 and 1994). The other maps have been drawn by Brian Connelly, from drafts prepared by J. H. Price, R. J. S. Wiseman and the late E. Beddard. Except for that of Neath, the maps refer to the electric tramway period, and not to the horse or steam tramways that preceded them.

The photographs include nearly thirty that have not been published before, including several taken in 1936 by the late G. N. Southerden. Photographs marked TMS are reproduced by permission of the Tramway Museum Society, from the R. B. Parr collection administered by the librarian at Crich, and those taken by the late Dr. H. A. Whitcombe are reproduced by courtesy of the Science Museum, London. Thanks are also due to A. D. Packer and Phil Trotter for their help in locating relatively unknown photographs, including the cover picture.

Periodicals consulted have included *Modern Tramway, Tramway Review, Modern Transport, Buses Illustrated, The Light Railway & Tramway Journal, The Tramway and Railway World, The Electrician, The B.E.T. Gazette* and the *South Wales Evening Post*. The references are listed in the order of their source value.

For the previously under-documented Swansea & Mumbles Railway, extensive use has been made by D. Beynon of the minute-books and other company papers now available for study in the library of University College, Swansea. Other material is held by the Swansea City Archivist and by West Glamorgan Central Reference Library. We also record our thanks to the reference librarians of Aberdare, Llanelli, Merthyr, Pontypridd and Rhondda for access to local maps and plans.

Bibliography — General

Great British Tramway Networks, by W. H. Bett and J. C. Gillham (Light Railway Transport League, 4th edition, 1962). The present work incorporates and expands the South Wales text of this book, which formed part of Chapter 8.

Keep Moving — The Story of Solomon Andrews and his Family, by J. F. Andrews (Stewart Williams, Barry, 1976). Describes horse tram operation in Cardiff, Llanelly, Newport, Pontypridd and Pwllheli.

Vintage Buses and Trams in South Wales, edited and published by Stewart Williams, Barry, 1975.

The Golden Age of Tramways, by C. F. Klapper (Routledge and Kegan Paul, 1961).

History of British Bus Services: South Wales, by David Holding and Tony Moyes (Ian Allan, 1985).

Aberdare

The Tramways of Aberdare, by R. J. S. Wiseman (in *Tramway Review* Nos. 129 to 133, 1987/8).

Tramway and Railway World, January 1914.

Article in *Buses Illustrated,* October 1966.

Cardiff

Cardiff's Electric Tramways, by H. B. Priestley, MA (in *Modern Tramway,* June to August 1940).

Cardiff's Electric Tramways, by D. Gould (Oakwood Press, 1974; second edition 1993/4).

Cardiff's Electric Tramways, by H. B. Priestley, MA (in *Tramway Review,* 84 to 93, 1975-8).

Modern Tramway, December 1942 (Introduction of flat fare).

Cardiff Service No. 9, by H. B. Priestley, MA (in *Trams* No. 9, April 1963).

Cardiff Corporation Transport Department Golden Jubilee brochure, 1952.

The Cardiff Trolleybus, 1942 to 1970, by D. G. Bowen and J. Callow (National Trolleybus Association, 1970).

City of Cardiff, 68 Years of Electric Transport, by D. G. Bowen (National Trolleybus Association, 1969).

Doodlebugs to Tiger Bay, by D. G. Bowen (in *Buses Illustrated,* April 1964).

The Cardiff Water Car, by I. L. Wright (in *Trams* No. 3, October 1961).

Modern Transport, 13 November 1943 and 5 April 1947 (Flat fares and PAYE).

Modern Tramway (Museum News), June 1986.

Tramway and Railway World, April 1923 and August 1927.

Ebbw Vale Funicular, 1992

Funicular Revival, Part 3 — Ebbw Vale, by J. H. Price (in *Light Rail and Modern Tramway,* May 1993).

Llanelly

Llanelly Trolleybuses, by G. Griffiths (Trolleybooks Joint Publications, 1993). Includes tramway chapter.

Trolleybus Magazine, July 1982 (article by G. L. Griffiths).

Trolleybus Systems — Llanelly, by A. G. Newman (in *Buses,* September 1975).

Modern Tramway, (Information Bureau), August 1942.

A Llanelli Chronicle, by Gareth Hughes (Llanelli Borough Council, 1984).

Merthyr Tydfil

The Tramways of Merthyr Tydfil, by J. Hathren Davies, 1937 (unpublished manuscript in Merthyr Library).

Tramway Review (Information Bureau), Nos. 115/6, 1983.

The Omnibus Magazine, November 1939 and January 1940.

50

Neath

Neath Corporation Tramways, 1897-1920, by Gordon Tucker (in *Tramway Review,* Nos. 107/8, 1981); additional information in issues 127/9 of 1986/7.

Article on gas trams in *Buses Illustrated,* April 1959.

Article in *Trams,* No. 26, July 1967.

Tramway and Railway World, 13 September 1917.

Neath & District — A Symposium, by Elis Jenkins (published by Author, 1974).

Newport

Trams and Buses of Newport, 1845 to 1981, by D. B. Thomas and E. A. Thomas (Starling Press, Newport, 1982).

Newport Trams, by Colin Maggs (Oakwood Press, 1977).

Newport Corporation Tramways, by B. H. Smith (in *Trams,* Nos. 11 and 12, 1963/4).

Modern Tramway (Information Bureau), July 1942.

Tramway and Railway World, June 1903 and April 1918.

Newport Transporter Bridge

Transporter Bridges, by N. N. Forbes (in *Modern Tramway,* February 1970; reprinted as a booklet).

Newport's Transporter Bridge, by L. G. Mayne (in *Meccano Magazine,* June 1959).

New Civil Engineer, February 1986.

Pontypridd

Passenger Tramways of Pontypridd, by R. Large (Oakwood Press, 1977).

Modern Tramway (Information Bureau), May 1941.

Trolleybus Systems — Pontypridd, by A. G. Newman (in *Buses,* February 1978).

Rhondda

Rhondda Transport Co. Ltd., Golden Jubilee brochure, 1956.

Article in *Trams,* No. 26, July 1967.

The Rhondda Valleys, by E. D. Lewis (1959), pages 126-9.

Trolleybus Systems — Rhondda, by A. G. Newman and C. I. Taylor (in *Buses,* April 1982).

Tramway and Railway World, June 1908 and January 1909.

Article in *Modern Transport,* 21 April 1956.

Swansea

Swansea's Electric Tramways, by H. B. Priestley, MA (in *Tramway Review,* Nos. 114-6, 1983).

Swansea Route No. 8 (Port Tennant), by H. B. Priestley, MA (in *Trams,* No. 8, January 1963).

1874 – 1937 (South Wales Transport Co. Ltd. commemorative brochure, 1937).

Tramway and Railway World, October 1899, September 1900, June 1912.

Swansea Constitution Hill funicular

A Tramway Fiasco, by J. H. Price (in *Modern Tramway*, December 1979).

Tramway and Railway World, November 1899.

Article by N. T. Wassell in *Red Dragon* (Railway Club of Wales magazine), March 1986.

Swansea and Mumbles

The First Passenger Railway, by C. E. Lee (Railway Publishing Co., 1942).

The Swansea and Mumbles Railway, by C. E. Lee (Oakwood Press, 1954).

Articles by C. E. Lee in *The Railway Magazine*, March/April 1929 and August 1954.

Articles in *Modern Tramway*, April 1942, November 1952, October 1959.

The Life and Times of the Swansea and Mumbles Railway, by Gerald Gabb (D. Brown & Sons, 1987). This book contains additional references and source notes to those listed here.

The Swansea & Mumbles Railway 1804-1904 Centenary Souvenir (Swansea Improvements and Tramways Co., 1904).

Mumbles Railway Centenary article in *B.E.T. Gazette*, August 1904.

The Swansea & Mumbles Cars, by G. Spink (in *Modern Tramway*, September 1965) with car drawing.

Electrification of the Mumbles Railway (South Wales Transport Co. Ltd., 1928).

Over 155 Years of Service (South Wales Transport Co. Ltd., 1960).

The Oldest Passenger Railway in the World (South Wales Transport Co. Ltd., 1954).

The Mumbles Railway (Mumbles Railway Society, 1981).

Swansea and Mumbles Trailers, by J. H. Price (in *Tramway Review* No. 21, Spring 1985).

South Wales Transport Co., by Alan Townsin and Chris Taylor (Transport Publishing Co., 1989).

Articles by Gerald Gabb in *Gower*, 1978 and 1980 (Gower Society).

Steam and the Mumbles Railway by F. Llewelyn Jones (Newcomen Society, 1980).

Journal of the Railway and Canal Historical Society, March 1981.

Brush Cars for the Mumbles Railway, 1928 (Brush Electrical Engineering Co.).

The Oldest Railway in the World (in *The Railway Magazine*, July 1908).

Rock & Roll to Paradise, by R. Gittings (Gomer Press, 1982).

The Tramway and Railway World, 16 May 1929.

Narrow Gauge Railways

Welsh Narrow Gauge Railways, by Peter Johnson (Railway World Special, Ian Allan 1991).

Fifteen Inch Gauge Railways, by D. Morley and P. van Zeller (includes Porthcawl).

Modern Tramway, April 1976 (Highfield Electric Tramway).

A Survey of Seaside Miniature Railways, by D. J. Croft (Oakwood Press, 1992).

Brecon Mountain Railway articles in *Railway World* November 1985 and *Steam Railway* April 1981 and November 1986.

Swansea-Mumbles Railway **150 YEARS OF SERVICE**

26 years of service by

From one horse power—derived mainly from oats !
—to the 100 h.p. of BTH-equipped cars, the Swansea-
Mumbles Railway has developed in size and speed.

Since 1928, BTH-equipped double-decker passenger
cars have maintained a fine tradition of reliability, and
are still good for many years of service.

BRITISH THOMSON-HOUSTON

THE BRITISH THOMSON-HOUSTON COMPANY LIMITED · RUGBY · ENGLAND

Member of the AEI group of companies

Printed in England in 1993 by W. J. Ray & Co. Ltd., Walsall WS1 2HQ for the Light Rail Transit
Association, 13A The Precinct, Broxbourne, Herts. EN10 7HY.   ISBN 0 948106 14 X.